I0198805

the
Spiral Sapling

the

Spiral Sapling

the poetry of
Karen Seyfert

EPIGRAPH BOOKS
RHINEBECK, NEW YORK

The Spiral Sapling: The Poetry of Karen Seyfert © 2020 by
Karen Seyfert

All rights reserved. No part of this book may be used or
reproduced in any manner without the consent of the
author except in critical articles or reviews. Contact the
publisher for information.

Hardcover ISBN 978-1-951937-84-3

Library of Congress Control Number 2020922651

Cover design by Kenneth W. Smith Jr.
Book design by Colin Rolfe

Epigraph Books
22 East Market Street, Suite 304
Rhinebeck, NY 12572
(845) 876-4861
epigraphps.com

This book is dedicated to my mother, Juanita, who gave me an ear for rhyme, to all the friends who listened and encouraged me, to daughters Lisa and Julie, and to my granddaughter, Bridget, who is the future.

CONTENTS

I - Discovering the Poet

II - Playing with the Sonnet

III – Afterwords

IV – Playing with Rhyme

I

DISCOVERING THE POET

MENTAL SPACE: WHAT IS IT?

It is writing a poem,
playing with images,
arranging words
on a page,
creating the universe.

It is knowing that
it is not required.
No one else needs me
to recreate the universe.

It is play
as God must have played,
choosing the song
for the wren.

TOUCHING THE EARTH

My father told me,
there is something sacred,
there is something healing
about touching the earth.
All of us animals knew once;
some have forgotten now.
They never walked barefoot
behind the plow, never
sank bare toes in cool mud,
never stretched, bone tired,
on bare ground at quitting time,
never felt the earth accept
the ache from the bones.

My father, farm boy, business man,
who started pulling calves late in life,
spent many a cold night in the cowshed
attending miracles, told me
cows lying on the earth
labored less, as though they lay
on the breast of the mother
and felt the rise and fall of her breath
replacing fear with peace.

My father, who once roped and
milked a cow for lunch,
who knows how to analyze

soil with his fingers,
who gets excited about irrigation systems,
who has always said "Yes," to life,
some distant day, will, I think,
lie down on the bare ground
as on the breast of the mother,
and peacefully, say "Yes,"
to death.

PROCRASTINATOR'S BLUES

Rolled out of bed
Tried to get crackin'
But I just couldn't raise my head.
I got the pro-cras-tin ator's blues,
An' that aint even news,
The pro-cras-tin-ator's, pro-cras-tin-ator's blues.

Last night after supper
Just like a lump I sat.
Didn' even like the TV,
But my getup was squashed flat.
I got the pro-cras-tin-ator's blues,
No one would ever choose,
The pro-cras-tin-ator's, pro-cras-tin-ator's blues.

I didn't make that phone call
An' now it's too late.
I didn't fold the laundry
Just wallowed in self hate.
I got the pro-cras-tin-ator's blues,
Please help me to refuse
The pro-cras-tin-ator's, pro-cras-tin-ator's blues.

So I say today'll be different,
I gotta get that big list done.
Oh Jesus, you gotta help me,
I aint havin' any fun.

I got the pro-cras-tin-ator's blues,
It's somethin' I gotta lose,
The pro-cras-tin-ator's, pro-cras-tin-ator's blues.

A RHYME FOR CARL

My husband went to work today;
he sat down in his chair.
His busy mind went straight ahead
As if I were not there.

He moved the continents about,
he probed the mountain ranges,
he toiled and danced from thought to thought
and dwelt upon Earth's changes.

The only sound the rustling page
and scribbles of the pen.
My husband will arm wrestle truth
until she must give in.

My husband went to work today;
there was not much to see,
for as with fish, ideas he'd play
with great dexterity.

He sits so still and quiet,
activity concealed.
He pounds and shapes upon the forge
ideas newly revealed.

At boulder truth he pounds 'till night.
Hard work yields little chips.
They're offered up with great delight
and smiles about the lips.

My husband went to work today;
he sat down in his chair.
The place where other husbands play,
my husband, he works there.

CARESS

The air, warm and humid
As a lover's body,
Had substance,
When you moved through it,
Like silk.

BLUE

Blue light of evening
After sunset, before dark
Children playing outside after dinner,
Twirling around
Falling down dizzy and laughing
Extracting the last sweetness from the day.
The clover chain is made
Long enough to encircle the house.
Soon the fireflies will be out
...first star I've seen tonight
wish I may, wish I might...

I wish that all children might have serenity,
Might have these moments available.
I wish nations might not harden their hearts,
Might give peace a chance.
Surely we have the skillsto negotiate.
Surely we know enough psychology.
Surely we negotiate from strength.
Let's not choose the blue smoke of war
And the red blood of children
Falling down.

JON BENET

Doll faced child
practiced sophisticated moves,
make up,
the beauty contest strut,
played at womanhood.

Woman, child, infant,
face of an angel
simmered with sexuality
and innocence,
the classic come on.

Jon Benet thrust into
a grown-up world
thrust into,
thrust into,
thrust into,
Death.

To us you are a tightness
in the back of the throat,
a burning behind the eyes.
We want to scream for you
and wail,
to enfold you and comfort.

But Mother God
has already kissed it
and made it well.

LOVE POEM

Side by side we go through life
Looking away in the same direction
Sharing quick shy glances
Embarrassed, awkward.
We hide behind screens,
Work, alcohol, TV, sex.
Like fan dancers, one fan drops
Another lifts so smoothly,
The flow is unbroken
The dance goes on.

Face to face turned into toe to toe;
It hurt. Embarrassed, awkward,
We remember to shift our gaze,
With practice we perfect the dance
It is smooth, unbroken, side by side.
It's OK.

But something in me longs for
person to person, heart to heart.
Almost I want our blood to flow
From person to person like shared
electrons around two bonded atoms.
I want to be known as close as breath.
I want to taste life with your mouth.

I want to be with you
Really.
I want to gaze into your eyes.
Lazily let us rest in each other's eyes,
Lovingly let us stop dancing,
Stand still and rest in the gaze
Until our souls step shyly out
And touch, and begin a new dance
Face to face.

I think heaven will start then
And I will not be hungry
And you will not be hungry
Any more.

FLIGHT

Driving,
Motor humming bass rhythms,
Me, keyed into the bass rhythms of everyday.
Without warning
I feel the familiar lift of the shoulders
As I take flight and soar.
I am also the long joyful wail of the vocalist
In the rock band.
And I know in that moment
All will be done...
Is being done.

POCKETS FULL OF GRAVITY

Pockets full of gravity,
serious stuff,
weigh us down with
"never enough."

Keys to the office,
house and shed,
lock all the doors
when you go to bed.

Need a computer,
a new cell phone,
washer's broken,
more things to own.

Heads full of gravity,
serious still,
tie our hands with
not until.

Blast off !
The life of the spirit
        is weightless!
                wait-less.

MEDICINE WHEEL

From this high holy place
at the windward edge
of the Bighorn Mountains
the spirit soars
into empty space
over western plains
and returns to dance the ring,
one with the forgotten ones
who created this wheel.
Spirit knows why
this place was chosen.
Here the weathered past.
Here the flowing future.
Here, the present wonder.
Hear.

MICE

Mouses in the wall,
Mouses in the hall,
Mouses in the trap,
Zappety zap zap.
Mouses on the floor
Dead as a door (nail).
Mouses in the gloom
Don't foretell our doom.
But....
Mouses in the spring
That's a nasty thing.
Mouses in the well?
Oh hell!

RANTING

I'm sad to say I feel that I
must now make myself scant.
I do not choose to be with you
and listen to you rant.

The world's not as it should be.
It's been thus since the Fall.
But I don't choose to listen to
complaints about it *all*.

A sorry word said now and then
I sure can tolerate.
But a constant stream of negatives
I've truly come to hate!

For there is so much that is good
it really isn't fair
that you ignore it just as though
it were not even there.

The sun is bright, the sky is blue,
the temperature is kind.
It is with simple positives
I choose to fill my mind.

You've every right to think your thoughts,
and yes to speak them too.
I'm sad to need a barrier
built up 'tween me and you.

SOMALIA 1993

Lord, how can I look at those pictures?
They tear at me.
The old man standing
straight,
once proud,
patiently waiting his ration,
ribs and bones looking like
Christ on a crucifix,
the essence of man
stripped of roundness or comfort.

Would that I could tear off some of my flesh
and give it to him!

How can I turn away?
I look out of the window.
Gentle flakes of soft snow
settle smoothly on the lawn,
a clean white blanket,
Serene.

Blanket…in those pictures
a Somali mother
had used one, not
so white or soft
but warmer, to wrap her child.

The child could no longer feel
the warmth of the scratchy wool.

A blanket is no refuge
from the sharp bones of reality.
Lord, how can I look at those pictures.

Music
    Sinks in
        Like gentle rain
            Into the ground.

I feel
    New buds open,
        Space
            For deep breath.

SAWYERS BAR CALIFORNIA

I'm sewing but there is no need
for frantic instrument of speed.
I hear the kettle singing on the fire,
the quiet pops and crackles from the stove,
And from the door
the white tossed river's muted roar.
Outside the window, houses? No,
but lofty mountain capped with snow.
The kettle whispers Shalom from the fire.
It knows that this is all I can desire.

LEO

Trees release golden leaves
no longer needed by the tree,
no longer required.
They served well during their time.
It is not for any breach of service
they are discharged.
Tumbling, they land lightly
on the stream surface.
But they are not finished;
they only make a change of duties
for the mother earth and the Father.

Leo used to help clean the grounds.
That was after he raised three children
all witnesses to the Father.
Tuesday he fell.
As softly as a leaf he let go
of this life and reached out for
a new set of duties,
for the mother earth,
and the Father he never forgot,
and who never forgot him.

GEORGE, AGE 94

George Morehead he gallantly gallops through life
with care for his family, employees, his wife.
Unfailingly thoughtful, new friends 'round him flock,
(They always acknowledge his age is a shock.)
For George and his Betty don't live in the past,
and age is no barrier when having a blast.
Their laughter infectious and rolicking too,
they're simply too busy now to be blue.
Young friends oft' prefer them to folks their own age,
the Moreheads are positive, lively, and sage.

Old George is a teacher. His subjects are three:
attentiveness, business, and plain courtesy.
But George may not know all the lessons he's taught,
for lessons, like passes, work best when they're caught.
From his actions shine values: look forward, work hard,
be responsible, faithful, don't let life be marred
by tragedies folks. The sun rises each day.
Get out there and meet it, you'd better make hay
while it's shining. Take notice of every new rose.
Let nothing escape you, for where the wind blows
we have no idea, and sure no control.
Plant feet wide on life's deck, and let the waves roll.

Keep galloping Georgie, we're cheering you on,
live life every minute until it is gone.

II

PLAYING WITH THE SONNET

THE SPIRAL SAPLING *or* INTERTWINED

Beside the path around the lake I found
a sapling grown to spiral when a vine
shared growing space with it. The tree was fine.
The vine had gone to nourish the rich ground.
The tree remembered how it had been bound.
I gazed at it and took it for a sign
of ways that lives shape lives, as yours has mine.
I hold your imprint though you're not around.
It comforts me to know you're with me thus.
Together we were not what would have been
if we'd not grown together but apart.
The world, and we would never have had "us".
Although no longer can that "us" be seen
I have you in my sinew and my heart.

NIAGARA

Niagara,
It used to be,
One hundred years ago,
We came to you
As to a shrine
And were overcome.
Niagara

Now, Niagara, we're
Saturated with images
From a big screen TV,
Barraged with hype,
Too busy for tranquility,
Embarrassed by awe.
We've crowded out wonder
Niagara.

 Now, Niagara
To get the peace we miss
We try alcohol.
To get the rush you gave us
We try cocaine,
And are driven harder
By these masters,
Niagara

Now, Niagara,
We fill our lives with busy-ness
To anesthetize the ache
Left by the gap you used to fill.
We never have enough
To get all the things
We think we need
From the mall,
Niagara

Please, Niagara,
Let us feel more
Than a flicker
Of the awe
You used to lavish
On us. Please,
Niagara.

Then, Niagara
We might guess
What has been missing.
We might make space
For tranquility
And time for wonder
To fill the gaps
Effectively,
Niagara.

LOVE BUGS – AN OXYMORON?

Some people may think the cicada's song is euphonius.
But we were tent camping, surrounded. It wasn't
 harmonius.

Maybe it can be at times when they've not been prolific.
When thousands of them scream all day and all night it's
 horrific.

When boys chased the girls with cicadas it wasn't
 salubrious,
And panicky girl's screams devolved into tears quite
 lugubrious.

Unable to turn the boys into some game less misogynist,
I wanted to stomp those bugs, squish them to something
 oleaginous.

Our actual form of revenge might seem sophomoric,
But feeding cicadas to ducks made us feel euphoric.

Note on Love Bugs:

Goals:

    To use the word list

    To tell a true story

    In Each couplet, a word from wordlist is used in the
        rhyme

    16 syllables per line (last 2 lines have 14 each)

After this I began to write sonnets.

Sliding under the wind,
Keeping the straight path
Under that whipping blanket,
Going to work.

SONNET FROM THE KEYS

Why does she sit in this exotic clime
within an RV smaller than her room.
Others get suntans, she prefers the gloom
before her laptop. There she spends her time.
She does not swim, sunbathe, or boating, climb
the mast. She will not fish. I must assume
she cares not where she is. The siren's tune
sings softly in her mind, and it's sublime.
"I write because I must honor the gift,
the sweet epiphany of poetry,
which comes unbidden as does grace to me.
Alone in quiet I create the lift
of wings and fly myself across the sea,
Ecstatic if the poem pleases me."

PAY ATTENTION

"The clearing was alive with blue," she said,
"One hundred bright blue buntings in my view,
and with them were two cardinals bright red.
I could not turn away or pass on through."
It hit her with the force of born again.
She called and told me, choking back the tears
her life work would be helping children win
a love of nature to enrich their years.
At sunrise every day the world's born new.
It glistens, shimmers, scintillates and sings;
the secret is that you must be there too.
Be not preoccupied with mundane things.
  To throw away these gifts is to live blind.
  Oh, Pay Attention, and fulfillment find.

KATRINA: THE SUBURBANITE'S REMORSE

Who will mourn the forgotten ones,
the ones who drowned in their attics
in the
Sanctity
of their own homes?

The invisible poor
who had the bad taste to
Affront us with their dead bodies
Floating
because they couldn't afford a car.

Or the more agile poor who were herded into the
Superdome and forgotten
until their toilets spilled onto the floor
a pestilence which tears were insufficient to wash away.

Residents of the nursing home
knew that the flow of life had passed them by.
With children busy with their own lives,
or far away, or dead, they had been
forgotten for months, years.
But then the flood found them
and thirty of them drowned, together
but alone.

Evacuation was the answer.
Those who were able made "the right choice"
taking their laptops, family photos, dogs, passports,
birth certificates, money, clothes and bedding.
Prudent folks, their cars were stuffed full
and slotted into the traffic lanes.

No room for another living soul
who was another color,
whose name was unknown,
who might even rob them.
Which of us prudent folk would have gone
Naked
into the
Unknown
with a carload of total strangers?

How they were to
Survive
was their problem.
There were so many details to remember.
No time to think of them.

Evacuation was the answer.
Why did governments forget,
that it was easier to get the forgotten ones
Evacuated
Before
than it was after the water rose?
How could they forget?

Those who govern live in the better neighborhoods
with the rest of those privileged to have the resources to
    survive.
Since domestic servants went out of style,
the people of color, the poor
have become ever more invisible.
We do not know them.
We forget for long periods
that they even exist.

Who will mourn the forgotten ones?
Those of us whose voyeuristic tendencies
have been titillated watching CNN.
Those of us whose consciences have been chaffed
a little, but not enough to change our lives,
can spare a moment of silence
on a national day of mourning.

PURPLE

The Indian speaker said,
"Purple is the color of danger
or opportunity,
the possibility of good or bad."
That afternoon I found a piece
of purple glass, beautiful, sharp edged;
I showed it to you. Later
we took new names and faces,
and became fifteen years old and
tormented by possibilities
of purple hue.

MY FATHER'S HORSE

My father's horse was sixteen hands tall.
She never walked, she pranced, knees lifted, neck arched.
Loosen the reins and she would gain momentum.
Lean forward, squeeze with your legs
and a power surge like a giant wave
would carry you flying forward.
Better twist one hand in her mane
and keep your weight over the stirrups
for you have released the caged lightning
and you can ride, ...you...can...ride
until you both are breathless,
she with racing, you with delight.

The power is yours, you hold it in your hands.
The massive dancing power is yours
and hers. She is never quite out of control.
If you can ride this one, you can ride
the whirlwind, you can ride life.

My father's horse is gone now,
but I'm still looking for the whirlwind
to prove that I can ride.

ON THE BEAT OF DRUMS

Soaring upward on the beat of drums,
celebrating the primitive,
heart pounding with the rhythm,
breath caught,
You materialized, apparition-like
out of the past.
We circled the fire and each other
and chanted.
As we left the circle together
suddenly I knew
the symbolism was much too vivid,
and so I gave up soaring
and plummeted back to the straight and narrow.
I let you read my poetry,
and that was all.

THE SKY IS CLOSED

The sky is closed.
The road is horizontal.
The gate is padlocked.
The store is out of it.
My mouth is closed.
The house is dark.
Lithium.
One hundred miles
through unremembered landscape
in the dark.
Cruise control.

The letter is unmailed.
The song is unwritten.
I maintain control.
The phone call not made.
The note not written.
The invitation not sent.
I maintain equanimity.
The guilt disallowed.

The trees are bare.
It is fall.
A time for holding.
A holding pattern.
The thruway is no place
for exploration.

AFTER 9-11 2001

It rained all day Friday and the bitter wind blew.
Just before sunset, God-light in the west
lit up vast reaches of the skies with rays.
It seemed like a symbol after the drear,
a reminder that we are not alone after all.
Really it's a cliché, used so often on greeting cards
and in movies just at this point, to show
hope and resolution after great trouble.

God-light, as though God could come down,
slide right down those slanted rays from heaven.
It's not true.
God doesn't live up in heaven.

However bad it is,
God doesn't need to visit.
God has been here all along.
When any of us cries for another's loss
God cries.
When people risk their lives to save another
God acts.
When someone suffers, God suffers.

When faced with death by fire or faling,
coworkers reached out, joined hands
and held tight as they jumped together,

from the World Trade Center.
No doubt God was there.

HOW SHALL I LIVE?

Gramps found her on the tennis court alone.
She sobbed, "I will be twenty soon and all
is changed. We watched our World Trade Towers fall,
now war. Might this be the next combat zone?
I'm not sure what is right. How is right known?
How shall I live?" He took a tennis ball
and bounced it hand to hand and off the wall.
He said, "Your trust in God is what you own
of value, and the pleasures of the earth;
treasure the small sweet moments of each day.
Consult the wise one in you and above.
Remember what you've learned of proven worth,
but don't let learning end. I know your ways
and you'll be fine. Be brave and act on love."

BEFORE THE DIAGNOSIS

The moment hangs suspended like a teardrop.
I move quietly about the kitchen
trying to create food sufficient
to the task of rejuvenation.
You breathe evenly on the couch,
sleeping, curled on your side.

I make comfort for myself, mixing and stirring,
watching you sleep.
It is not as active as hoping.
It is trusting way down deep
and holding steady,
cradling the stillness.

THE DOCTOR'S WAITING ROOM

The doctor's waiting room,
rows of chairs along the walls
below pastel landscapes, nicely framed,
tables strewn with glossy magazines.
On one cover a glamorous pregnant
woman in a bare red dress,
on another a fairy tale beautiful child.
None of these attract me.
I look around at the ordinary folks
waiting in the chairs,
people with health worries and
bills to pay.
They had to get off work to come here.
One woman greets her granddaughter
who came to wait with her,
"Don't kiss me…I love you."
Another turns to her husband,
"One article in this whole thing is reality.
The others is just not in my world."

HIKING OUT

Dust bloomed above the trail with each foot fall,
coated our calves and filtered through our socks.
Beside us lay the emerald pools, the rocks
and riffles of the stream whose siren's call
ignored, we hurried on, full packs and all.
My mind rushed on ahead to fresh clean frocks,
and baths, and beds with sheets, and the mail box,
and restaurant food, and shopping in the mall.
For even though we chose the wilderness
as summer's home and reveled in its joys,
we craved reunion with the common things
we in our daily lives would not call bliss.
There, we disdain civilization's toys
and long to hear how the wild river sings.

HESITATION STEP

The hesitation step
Practiced for our wedding
An odd ceremonial pace
Soon abandoned.

He taught me the long stride
Designed to cover ground quickly
I learned to love the stretching,
Reaching, feel of it,
The way the ground passed under our feet,
The directness and power.

I still choose to walk beside him
But now....
    the hesitation...
       step...
is a way of...
    life,
accompanied by...
      unexpected...
moments for meditation.
I can learn to love these also.

WHY SONNETS?

He majored in science, minored in math,
quick and creative, Stanford PhD.
In field-work long sure strides covered the path,
his movements agile as his mind, and free.
Did you know Parkinsons affects the mind?
As if a slow stiff body weren't enough.
Now what to tip the wait staff's hard to find,
and walking, sitting straight up, those are rough.
He freezes as if locked into a vault,
his mind jams like his body, with no plea.
But this great soul, persistent to a fault
will not complain, has never asked, "Why me?"
His wife, as all around her falls apart,
needs structured sonnets to create her art.

PSALM

We praise you, God, we offer you our joyful praise,
you can keep us at peace in the eye of the hurricane,
you are the rock of safety in the foaming rapids.
We praise you, God of constancy.

With eyes fixed on you we walk the tightrope
between allowing and uncaring.
God of balance and wholeness,
you see us watching our feet on the stepping stones
and call us to be the figure skater who spins and
spins and keeps her balance by turning her head
always keeping her eyes on one spot.
When our eyes are fixed on you, you keep us from falling.
We praise you, God of balance.

In the day your world glistens in the sunlight,
It rains and the earth gratefully drinks it in.
In the darkness, the stars fill us with delight,
we curl up in the warmth of your love for restful sleep.
We praise you, God of order and goodness.

Lord of Glory, you have scattered glory onto the
     sparkling snow
and onto the faces of your children in loving
     relationships.
Lord of love, you have shared your love,
in the homes of friends, the wagging tails of dogs,

the unconditional love of families, the kindness of
strangers.
We praise you, God of Love and Glory.

Oh, let our praises be unending.
Let them well up from our hearts and overflow upon your
earth
and on all of your creation, in acts of kindness.
Glory to you, God, for you will make us whole.

HOME

Old pleasures
Crisp fall air and
The colors of leaves
Old china and silver
The table set carefully
Vase of flowers at the center
Making beauty, comfort, peace
Silence or thoughtful conversation
Smell of good food cooking
Eye contact with friends
Order most beautiful
Fireplace glowing
Cat on your lap
Then our bed
Snuggling.

A DIFFERENT PALATE

Returned again to New York's early spring
after the color saturated Keys
where flowers never think about a freeze
and spill bright colors in a Lenten fling.
The waters there with turquoise and mauve sing
anthems for eyes that bring us to our knees,
and thankfulness caresses with the breeze.
Here, painters must a softer palate bring.
The world is gray, pale blue and hues of brown,
and rust and dark red stems relieve the eyes
for beauty-seekers tuned to subtlety.
Oh, be like evergreens, wear beauty's gown
through drab days waiting for late spring's surprise.
Hydrangeas, yet, will host the bee.

WHITE HERONS

April 11, 2002
The morning light is plain like cold water.
…What do I feel like wearing
since there's no place to go, and
shall I finish that job today?
Before you got sick, you used to do the taxes.
You were good at it.

I rinse the breakfast dishes.
Every moment away from the taxes feels illicit.
I have waited too long. Even so
I cannot sit interminably, staring at the page.
I look up. I want flowers for the vase.
Maybe there is something early in the yard.

Hyacinths, too few of them, grow by the door.
Crocus blossoms, radiant in seeming perfection,
bloom under the trees.
I mourn for those bruised by careless feet.
I know the perfect thing, pussy willows.
Some have grown back from the stump
where we tried to hack them into oblivion.
I need the clippers, and go back into the house.
I can't find them,
then forget the flowers.

April 12, 2002
I wake up to a brilliant sun and a still unfinished task.
I had hoped to be done by today so I could go outside,
but I'm not.
Get it over with!
not carelessly, meticulously.

You get it into your head that you must go fishing
and I must drive you there, fifty miles
to the Cattaraugus Reservation.
I try to refuse.
Over the motor I voice my frustration
at the interruption in the face of the feared deadline,
over and over, until I tire of hearing my Unpleasant Self.

While you fish I decide to wait by napping in the car.
Partly I'm tired, partly rebellious.
I hear the spring peepers as I snuggle into the back seat
and sleep.

I wake to your call, instantly all attention,
Are you in trouble? Do you need me?
I run down the path to the riverbank.
Beaming, you show me two white herons
downstream on the opposite bank.
Luminous.
We count the decades we have lived
in western New York without this sighting.

I'm happy to see them.
I could walk down the gravel road alongside the river
and get a closer look. Instead I retreat to the car.

and pick up the magazine I brought.
There's an article about the decline of direct nature study
in our schools and our lives,
how we are more and more estranged from the planet.

A little abashed, I decide it's time to walk down the road
and look for the herons.
The extraordinary birds are gone.
I could almost doubt they were ever there.
Further down the gravel road I stop to listen
to little streamlets, inches wide.
They sound exactly like
the dear rainy-weather pasture creek of my childhood.

The purple stems of wild brambles crisscross
deep red stems of red osier dogwood
and dried stems of teasle, asters and goldenrod.
Images of their summer glory crowd the present.
There is the surprising greenness of ground-hugging
    herbs,
which stay green all winter under the snow.
I catch the smell of mint and damp moss.

I move slowly, yielding to the moment.
The peepers are irrepressible now but cannot overpower
the silence growing within.
The herons have flown but in their place are two
dark-haired women from the reservation.
I think of calling to them, asking if they saw the herons,
but the silence is too precious to break.

Walking back to the car I recognize
I am on the Seneca Reservation and
The whole thing resembles a native tale
in which two white herons appeared
to be spirit guides for me
before changing back to young women.

III

AFTERWORDS

WALTZING WITH WORDS

Computers press words down into a straight line.
With an effort Words tolerate it;
They would rather dance.
They want to do loops and barrel rolls
Bouncing off the page before our transfixed gaze,
Our open-mouthed stare.

"We didn't know they could do that,"
We say, lying a little. We did know but forget.
"Maybe it was my imagination" we think
after we blink our eyes.

Volume we turn up, lets strike up the band,
Words won't sit still under my writing hand.
Oh Halleluia! Oh isn't this grand!
Flying and flipping words circle our stand,

Swooping and Looping we're waltzing with words,
Flowers and towers those fairytale words.
Oh help me to catch them before they move on,
 Be gentle, they're fragile,
        Oh... now they are gone.

HERE I AM STILL

He died.
The one who gave me that first kiss
when I was 15,
who held my hand in the movies,
who slipped a ring on my finger.
It had a diamond clear enough to walk around inside.
He gripped my hand as I labored to birth each child.
He planted trees in our yard.
They grew to heights we hadn't imagined.
And then, the bounce was gone from his walk.
How could he be bent over like that?
I have to take care of him now.
My husband!
He died.

I had and had not seen it coming.
I thought, "I have had a good life.
It is enough.
I really don't need more."

But the sun kept rising.
Here I am, still.
What is to be done?
Nothing much is left to do.
I fall asleep over my reading.
Nothing much to get up for.
He needed me.

Who needs me now?
God? ....God.
Even now.

I am starting to wake up,
to imagine possibilities,
slowly, like learning to read.

DAD'S LAUGH LINES

I remember when I first discovered that
the laugh lines around your eyes were fixed.
I accused you of harboring some secret joke
Which you were not ready to share.
You denied it.
Instead of discovering a secret that day,
I discovered the benevolent pleasure
With which you viewed life,
The incipient smile ready to break forth,
The "Yes."

Note: My father's memoir is called *Yes by George*.

LAST TRIP

Driving
the motor home cross country with my father,
who is finally old at one hundred three,
is doing battle on all fronts:
fighting wind, traffic jam, lane switchers, the cold,
November's shortened light, darkness.

In constant attendance, I have
concern for neck pain, the knee that gives away,
stomach upset, exhaustion, regularity, the state of
the diaper. Is he drinking enough?

I am hopelessly outflanked.

It *is* November.
Sometimes the cold creeps into his legs and they will
not warm. He says he is going to quit fooling around
with eating, says it's too much trouble to go on.

Death follows like a big truck bearing down.
We speed on to the next destination,
Trying to forget the final one.

PINES

Sheets of sunlight do not pour into my yard.
The sun comes broken and dappled
onto the moss and needle carpet, or the snow.
There is always a place to stand in the shade
with your face toward the sun
and watch how the pines handle sunlight.

The sun behind a hardwood's broader leaves
makes them glow translucent with intense color.
Pine needles remain opaque.
The light slides off their surface.
It splatters; is spun into strands,
like spider webs of blown glass.
Droplets of pure light imitate the sun.
I am dazzled.

Unlike hardwoods, pines are constant.
Oh they bow down under heavy snow
or ice, but they remain ravishing.
Last winter during a thaw, I watched the glittering
ice cascade from their branches until the shards
littered the snow like fallen stars.

No wonder I forgive the pines
for all the times I have to stoop
or crane my neck to see the moon.

XENOLITH

A xenolith is a rock from outside,
the Latin roots mean stranger-rock he said,
into the magma chamber it did slide
and drifted down into the molten red.
We dropped our packs and stared at the black stone
encased in granite, white with small black flecks.
With knife sharp edges this piece fell alone
from magma chamber's roof to slow vortex.
Within the molten mass this fragment failed
to melt Its edges are still sharp and straight.
Although by errant elements assailed,
it settled, but would not assimilate.
Remember, writ in stone now we can see
this fine example of integrity.

THE WIDOW'S WINTER EVENING

After dinner
when the drowse creeps on her
she yields
settles down on the couch
pulls up the afghan
makes room for the cat.
After a while she notices
sweetly that she has not heard
the radio program end.
Another music is on now
No reason to move.
The music slips in and out of
her awareness several times
comfortably like an old friend
stepping out the back door
and back in without knocking.
Delicious stillness undisturbed.

Only when the cat taps her face
with that gentle repetition
does she think "Is it morning?"
Softly the evening's indulgence
is recalled.
Stretching luxuriously
she smiles
opens her eyes.

Too late to call her cousin.
She knows without looking.
Cousin Pat also lives alone
and is in bed often before nine.

But, when they are together
there is a feast of conversation,
a wave that carries them
seamlessly onto the shore of
midnight, before
smiling with surprise,
these two old ladies
notice the hour and
make their way to bed.

POOR THING

My mother read to me from our small collection of
   children's books.

> "The North wind doth blow and soon we'll have
>   snow,
> And what will poor robin do then, poor thing?
> He'll sit in a barn and keep himself warm
> And hide his head under his wing, poor thing."

I always asked, "Why does it say 'poor thing',
mommy?" I would have been sitting in a big deep
armchair next to my mother in front of the fire. The floor
lamp beside us would have been casting a golden glow
on the page. Through the windowed walls on either side
of the fireplace I could see, in the cold blue twilight, the
leafless forest.

Why does it say, 'poor thing'?

One night in Wyoming, snow and high wind beat
against my father's house isolated in the fields. There
was not a tree, nothing to break the wind. Darkness
had fallen, we could see very little outside the picture
windows. The living room was warm and bright, the fire
was cheerful on the hearth. A small bird flew against the
window pane, repeatedly fluttering its wings against the
glass, trying to get in, poor thing. The next morning I
found the little bird dead on the porch.

Why is it always, 'poor thing'?

"Why does it say "Poor thing", Mommy?
It always says "Poor thing"?
I don't like being sad, Mommy?
Just go away sadness" I'd sing.

My mother, would snuggle me up in her arms
and rock back and forth in our chair.
She told me a story of my cousin Pat.
"Remember how she braids her hair?
Each side is divided in three equal parts,
You can't have a braid without three.
Well life's like that braid.
One part's sadness, one's joy,
and love is the third part," said she.
"They're twisted together to make up the braid.
Without sadness, it simply cannot be made....
You know after winter there always comes spring;
And then, if you listen, the wood thrush will sing."

All through that wise counsel I made not a peep
By the time she was finished, I was fast asleep.

JOY

It's Joy that I'm talking about, not pleasure,
not sweet content, but full fledged, all out joy.
Memory proves it a precious treasure
although it happened when you were a boy.
When hearing music made you want to shout,
when double rainbow took your breath away,
when at the mossy spring you filled your cup,
Some call it "flow," Carl said, "A Golden Day."
The Celtic Christians called some places thin,
believed from there heaven was not so far.
I think it's more the moment that you're in
and love and beauty help to lift the bar.
One thing seems true while I'm yet on Earth's sod,
when lifted up by joy, we're close to God.

A FRESH BLESSING

In brilliant sun,
every leaf cupped droplet
reflects,
mirrors,
sparkles.
Shining, rain slicked leaves
flip and
twist downward,
to the waiting earth.
Every one a fresh blessing.

RUST AND TIME

The sound of rust and time might be
the rattle of a sagging gate
chained loosely shut,
in the wind.
Should it be silent? No.
There will be eternity for that.
You might hear laughter in the squeak and rattle
 if you threw down your own sadness.
 Listen, can't you hear it?
Is it laughing at the calendar?
or something else, maybe the rust?
One can still go in and out through this gate.
The view through the bars is something
familiar once, and still attractive.

EXHORTATION

This is your life, nobody else's.
Do you really want to spend it
waiting, around.
The sun is up, where are you?
What are you avoiding? Better live it.

"But I don't know how."

                    Baloney.
Begin. There is no map.
Start with the outrage
you feel. Go ahead, feel it. I
know it hurts. Stay with it.
You will survive. Think of those
who have not survived.

You think your privilege will
keep you safe? Will it excuse you
from the life to which you are called.
Called, impelled, mandated,
pricked, pushed, begged to take up.
What does it profit you to gain
the whole world and lose that life?

You will go where you cannot imagine.
Godspeed.

SUNDAY MORNING WORSHIP

No need to light candles.
The flood of sunshine into the house
after so many cloud oppressed mornings
is enough to make thankfulness effortless.
It comes with joyful connection with God.
This beginning of Advent, on Zoom,
I felt love for my church friends
and the love of my church people
for each other.
Our Pastor preached, "It would be a shame to
waste a perfectly good crisis."
And we have not.

I am still worshiping. The air is different.
This almost never happens.
Cleaning my house has taken on the
cast of holiness. Cleaning the toilet
has taken on the aspect of holy service.
Reaching out has become a sacramental
imperative accepted with Joy.

Two blue jays are sitting on my gutter
tossing a shower of leaves in front of my window.
This is the third miracle of the morning.
Cleaning the gutter is today's preordained task.
The first miracle was my brief awakening
timed precisely for Moonset and awe.

These are added to the quality of light
and the persistence of worship.

Today's advent word is Hope,
and gratitude has opened the door.
Thank you.

IV

PLAYING WITH RHYME

COYOTE SONG

Chorus: From Brother Coyote there's nothing to fear.
   Like all of Earth's creatures he has a right to be
      here.

Five little coyotes lived in the field next door;
Some people built a house there, and then there were
   four.

Four little coyotes were happy running free;
One ate poisoned meat and then there were three.

Three little coyotes got the garbage we threw;
One swallowed a steel fork, and then there were two.

Two little coyotes crossed the road in the sun,
Along came a fast car and then there was one.

One little coyote all alone, feeling blue,
Up trots his new girlfriend, and then there were two.

Two little coyotes in love and alive,
One morning in spring time, well, then there were five.

The farmer's young family watched them play round
   their den,
Enjoyed and decided to speak up for them.

Repeat Chorus

THE KINKAJOU

Let's think about the Kinkajou,
although she hardly thinks of you.
She lives high in rainforest trees
among the butterflies and bees.
She's sometimes called the honey bear,
she loves the honey she finds there,
her fur is honey colored too,
the soft and furry kinkajou.

She's really not a bear at all.
The kinkajou is rather small,
in fact, she's smaller than my cat.
She could curl up inside my hat.
In South America she lives
and to her relatives she gives
A taste of juicy tropic fruit.
The kinkajou is pretty cute.

She climbs so quickly, with such ease
it's like she's running up the trees.
To hold the tree, on all four paws
the kinkajou has big long claws.
She climbs straight up, she climbs straight down.
Her tail she uses curled around
 the branches, so if claws should slip
she doesn't even lose her grip.

Big eyes face front and help her see
how long the jump from tree to tree.
But most amazing is her knack
of turning her feet front to back.
With front-back feet, the kinkajou, she knows,
whichever way she wants to go...she goes.

It rains a lot, her world is wet,
but she is happy there, you bet.
The rain forest grows lots of fruit.
With bugs and insects it will suit
to feed mom and dad kinkajou.
The babies drink milk when they're new.
Their mommies keep them safe up high
when winds blow their trees round the sky.

Say bye-bye to the kinkajou
until one day you might go too
to visit the rain forest trees,
and there, if you say pretty please
you might just see a kinkajou.
The kinkajou just might see you.
And then when you've gone someplace new
the kinkajou might ... think of you.

BEAVER

Whoever thought the beavers
would ever be so clever
to be the best of weavers
with branches and with sticks.

They build their dam so neither
the dry or stormy weather
can change the water level
in ways they cannnot fix.

The dam is their creation.
Its mud and stone foundation
a flood cannot dishevel
and winter cannot nix.

In winter the mud freezes
and this the beaver pleases.
The dam is even stronger
with ice within the mix.

Their lodge is built of branches
and mud, just like some ranches
that people call adobe
and build with sundried bricks.

Their door is underwater
but beaver's sons and daughter

are dry and warm in winter
on a raised floor of sticks.

The birch or poplar either
are trees that please the beaver
for building dams and lodges
and munching twigs and bark.

So come and see the beaver.
You'll find them now in either
a place called Beaver Meadow
or in your wetland Park.

BUG LOVE

It used to be
That when I'd see a bug
I'd just say "Ugh!"

And day or night
I just felt fright
I thought they'd bite.

It's different now
Because I see
Most insects mean
No harm to me.

Insects found now
Make me say "Wow!"
Their shapes, their ways
Surely amaze.

They dig, they swim,
They fly, they crawl,
But that's not all.

They walk on water,
Hide in spittle,
Some have long legs,
Some have little.

They change their shapes
And habitats.
What do you really think of that?

They're brown all over
Or colored bright,
Some even make
Their own soft light.

For life's small things
Can fascinate
If we can just
Forget to hate.

URSUS INTERRUPTUS

On our way to Ouray we bought cherries to share
Never thought what we bought would be eaten by bear.

To unload the car, we turned our backs for a minute.
We didn't go far… but the bear got in it.

From the porch Gretchen warned, "A bear is near,"
When Julie came out to gather more gear.

Julie stuck her head in almost close enough to kiss
The bear, interrupted, who gave a loud hiss.

Back on the porch, the gals stood aghast
And wondered how long his visit would last.

Julie took out her phone to call 9-1-1,
But the bear decided it had had enough fun.

It jumped from the car and they shouted "Hooray"
Bears belong in the woods and not in Ouray.

BEAR LIMERICK

There once was a bear from Ouray
Who smelled cheese in a car blocks away
Climbed into the seat
And was surprisingly neat
At eating the lunch from the day.

WHAT THE PTARMIGAN SAID

In camouflage I can hide
Even though I am outside.
Look right at me, you won't see
Where I'm hiding, clever me.
Colors speckled like the light
Hide me even in plain sight.

Hide and seek, for you a game,
But for me it's not the same.
You play with friends, four or five.
Hiding helps me stay alive.
I am living on my own
Please don't chase, leave me alone.

BRIDGET IS NINE

Bridget is our hero
and also our friend.
She once was age Zero,
now Nine. There's no end
of things she can do now:
ski mountains, climb rocks,
make cupcakes (she knows how),
do dances, track fox.

I watch how she's growing
these 3,285 days.
I'm happy she's knowing
so many good ways
to be a fine girl
and be nine in the world.
She has met the test.
Our Bridget is the best.

www.ingramcontent.com/pod-product-compliance
Lightning Source LLC
Chambersburg PA
CBHW020449100426
42813CB00031B/3309/J